YOU WILL BE A GREAT GOLFER

You Will Be a Great Golfer

Read Daily for Affirmation Book Series

Walter the Educator

Silent King Books

SILENT KING BOOKS

SKB

Copyright © 2024 by Walter the Educator

All rights reserved. No part of this book may be reproduced in any manner whatsoever without written permission except in the case of brief quotations embodied in critical articles and reviews.

First Printing, 2024

Disclaimer
This book is a literary work; poems are not about specific persons, locations, situations, and/or circumstances unless mentioned in a historical context. This book is for entertainment and informational purposes only. The author and publisher offer this information without warranties expressed or implied. No matter the grounds, neither the author nor the publisher will be accountable for any losses, injuries, or other damages caused by the reader's use of this book. The use of this book acknowledges an understanding and acceptance of this disclaimer.

I pray that you will be a great golfer.

For where two or three are gathered together in my name, there am I in the midst of them – Matthew 18:20

YOU WILL BE A GREAT GOLFER

Beneath the azure skies, where emerald fields expand,

You Will Be A GREAT GOLFER

I tread with purpose, a golf club in my hand.

You Will Be A GREAT GOLFER

Whispering winds applaud my questing heart,

You Will Be A
GREAT
GOLFER

Each blade of grass, a witness to my start.

You Will Be A GREAT GOLFER

With dawn's first light, I rise, resolve renewed,

You Will Be A GREAT GOLFER

A symphony of dreams, in morning dew imbued.

You Will Be A
GREAT
GOLFER

The rolling hills, the sand traps, and the greens,

You Will Be A
GREAT
GOLFER

My canvas vast, where passion intervenes.

You Will Be A
GREAT
GOLFER

I will be a great golfer, hear my solemn vow,

You Will Be A
GREAT
GOLFER

Through practice, patience, and the sweat upon my brow.

You Will Be A GREAT GOLFER

No challenge too daunting, no obstacle too high,

You Will Be A
GREAT
GOLFER

I will conquer the course, beneath the boundless sky.

You Will Be A
GREAT
GOLFER

The tee box beckons, where my journey starts,

You Will Be A
GREAT
GOLFER

A single stroke to chart the course of hearts.

You Will Be A
GREAT
GOLFER

With each swing, I channel nature's force,

You Will Be A
GREAT
GOLFER

My spirit merging with the golf ball's course.

You Will Be A
GREAT
GOLFER

The driver in my hand, a wand of might,

You Will Be A
GREAT
GOLFER

Launching dreams into the azure height.

You Will Be A
GREAT
GOLFER

The fairway stretches, a path both straight and wide,

You Will Be A
GREAT
GOLFER

Guiding me onward, with every stride.

You Will Be A
GREAT
GOLFER

Bunkers lie in wait, with treacherous embrace,

You Will Be A
GREAT
GOLFER

But I face them boldly, with a steady pace.

You Will Be A
GREAT
GOLFER

For in each challenge, opportunity lies,

You Will Be A
GREAT
GOLFER

To grow, to learn, to reach for skies.

You Will Be A
GREAT
GOLFER

The rough may threaten, with its tangled snare,

You Will Be A
GREAT
GOLFER

But I will navigate, with skill and flair.

You Will Be A
GREAT
GOLFER

For in my heart, a fire burns bright,

You Will Be A
GREAT
GOLFER

To be a great golfer, to reach the height.

You Will Be A
GREAT
GOLFER

On the green, the flag stands tall and true,

You Will Be A GREAT GOLFER

A beacon guiding me, as dreams accrue.

You Will Be A
GREAT
GOLFER

With putter poised, I judge the subtle slope,

You Will Be A
GREAT
GOLFER

The ball rolls smoothly, fulfilling hope.

You Will Be A
GREAT
GOLFER

A whispering cheer, a quiet sigh of peace,

You Will Be A GREAT GOLFER

As the ball drops in, finding sweet release.

You Will Be A
GREAT
GOLFER

For every hole achieved, a milestone passed,

You Will Be A
GREAT
GOLFER

A testament to goals pursued steadfast.

You Will Be A
GREAT
GOLFER

I will be a great golfer, this I know,

You Will Be A
GREAT
GOLFER

With each swing taken, with each seed sown.

You Will Be A
GREAT
GOLFER

For greatness lies in every step we take,

You Will Be A
GREAT
GOLFER

In every chance we grasp, in every break.

You Will Be A
GREAT
GOLFER

YOU WILL BE A GREAT GOLFER

ABOUT THE CREATOR

Walter the Educator is one of the pseudonyms for Walter Anderson. Formally educated in Chemistry, Business, and Education, he is an educator, an author, a diverse entrepreneur, and he is the son of a disabled war veteran. "Walter the Educator" shares his time between educating and creating. He holds interests and owns several creative projects that entertain, enlighten, enhance, and educate, hoping to inspire and motivate you.

> Follow, find new works, and stay up to date
> with Walter the Educator™
> at WaltertheEducator.com

www.ingramcontent.com/pod-product-compliance
Lightning Source LLC
LaVergne TN
LVHW051921060526
838201LV00060B/4115